Haikus

By

Princetonians

2018–2019

Edited by Mayumi Itoh

In memory of

Marius B. Jansen

Contents

Foreword

Among the genres of poetry that have travelled abroad and into new languages around the world, perhaps none has been so triumphant as the Japanese *haiku*. The lyricism, brevity, and potential wit of the form make it accessible to even the youngest poets, as many parents of American schoolchildren know; in more complex versions, its aesthetics of evocation can make it challenging for even the most experienced of writers. This collection of haiku composed in Japanese and translated into English offers readers the work of eight Princeton students, led by their advisor, Professor Mayumi Itoh, who met nine times over the course of the academic year 2018-2019 to learn the rules and conventions of this popular poetic genre. The results you find here reveal both the commitment of the students and the talent of their teacher.

As the organization of the collection shows, seasonality—the rhythm of the natural year, here divided into calendar months—is the foundation of traditional haiku in Japanese. But unlike seasonality in English poetry such as Keats's "To Autumn," for example, which explores a long series of scenes and metaphors for the season, the haiku poet is limited to seventeen syllables (or *morae*), divided into three lines of five, seven, and five. The poet therefore can only gesture towards the quality of a particular moment through images that invoke specific moods, sensations, or views. Take, for example, this haiku from "February," by Felicity Audet: 千鳥から/白い世界に/音のなし "In the white world/ there is no sound/ from the plover." Rather than describing a bird in a snowy landscape, Audet deftly harnesses absence to suggest a natural world that has been both silenced and stilled by winter. Each of the haiku here employs a particular "season word" or phrase that is associated with winter, spring, summer, or autumn, and each poet here has made unique choices about the weight and power of that word in their respective compositions. In Jacob Williams's haiku in "July," for example, the season word for summer heat (*hi zakari*) transforms everything visible and sensible into mirage: 日盛りや/ 地が無定形/ 空となる "At the hottest time of the day / the earth is shapeless/ and becomes air." Thanks to the efforts of Professor Itoh and the students, the haiku here appear in four versions, with kanji, hiragana, katakana, romanization, and in English, giving readers both linguistic and literary lessons.

Professor Itoh has kindly dedicated the collection to the memory of Professor Marius Jansen (1922-2000), Professor of Japanese history at Princeton and one of the founding members of the department first known as Oriental Studies and later the Department of East Asian Studies. Certainly this collection demonstrates that Princeton's current program in Japanese language and culture continues to be lively and engaged well beyond the classroom, inspiring students, and carrying on the work of its many distinguished faculty members and alumni.

--Anna M. Shields, Acting Chair and Professor of East Asian Studies

List of Photographs

All photographs were taken by the editor.

Photograph 1. Snow-covered branches

Photograph 2. Frozen Lake Carnegie

Photograph 3. Pear blossoms

Photograph 4. Cherry blossoms in the rain

Photograph 5. Bleeding heart flowers

Photograph 6. "Water Lilies and Japanese Bridge (1899)"

by Claude Monet, Princeton University Art Museum

Photograph 7. Seashells

Photograph 8. Sunflowers

Photograph 9. Sunset reflections on Lake Carnegie

Photograph 10. Ivy fall foliage

Photograph 11. Maple fall foliage on the snow

Photograph 12. Winter sun

Notes on the Text

This anthology comprises about 100 haikus that were written by students at Princeton University. This work categorized them according to the twelve months and the four seasons (plus the "new year" which constitutes an independent 'season' because of its importance to Japanese culture). This book presents each haiku in both Japanese and English so that non-Japanese-speaking readers can fully appreciate them. The text is formatted so that the first page for a given haiku (on the left side) shows the original haiku in Japanese, which is made up of a combination of Chinese characters (*kanji*) and Japanese phonetic characters (*hiragana* and *katakana*).

Then, in order to facilitate a better understanding, especially for those who are studying Japanese, the original haiku is shown in a modern spelling only in *hiragana* and *katakana*. This allows readers to see how the haiku is exactly pronounced phonetically. There are many ways to pronounce specific *kanji* words, and the original Japanese haiku does not indicate how each *kanji* character is actually pronounced. Afterward, the identification of the season word—an essential element in haiku—for the haiku is given.

On the second page for a given haiku (on the right side), a romanization of the original Japanese haiku is provided, first, so that English-speaking readers can understand how the haiku is pronounced. The words in Roman letters are divided into smaller groups of syllables, for easier reading. Then, an English translation of the haiku is presented. Due to the grammatical differences between English and Japanese, the word order of the haiku in English might be different from that of the original haiku in Japanese. It is followed by the English translation of the season word. This completes the presentation of a given haiku.

For romanizing Japanese words, the Hepburn style is primarily used, with macrons. However, macrons are not used for words known in English without macrons, as for Kyoto and Tokyo. Another exception is that "n" is not converted to "m" for words where it precedes "b, m, and p." Examples include tonbo (dragonfly), instead of tombo; sanma (Pacific saury), instead of samma; and tanpopo (dandelion), instead of tampopo. Enjoy!

Acknowledgements

In publishing this haiku anthology written by students at Princeton University, I would like to express my sincere appreciation to the University's Japanese Students Association (JSA) former president Kouta Ohyama and incumbent president Shiina Yuri for providing the opportunity to create a haiku workshop and for making a reservation for the classroom for each session.

I would also like to thank the Department of East Asian Studies Japanese Language Program director Shinji Sato and lecturers Tomoko Shibata, Hisae Matsui, and Yukari Tokumasu, as well as acting department chair Anna Shields, for their generous support and promotion of this haiku workshop. I also thank Greg Rewoldt and Meg Itoh for their continuous help.

The workshop met nine times during the 2018–2019 academic year and a total of 11 students participated in it.

This anthology is the result of their hard work and lively discussions.

In addition, this anthology is a memorial tribute to Marius B. Jansen, who established the Japanese Language Program at what has become the Department of East Asian Studies of the university and mentored countless students. Although I was not a student at the university, he extended generous tutelage to me and helped me launch an academic career in this country. Publishing this book is a minuscule way of repaying my deep indebtedness to this great scholar and educator.

Mayumi Itoh

キャンパスの
　　蔦の葉の聴く
　　　講義かな

On the campus
　　the ivy leaves are listening
　　　　to the lecture

January

Photograph 1. Snow-covered branches

初茜

　　星だけと見た

　　　　朝の色

はつあかね

　　ほしだけとみた

　　　　あさのいろ

季語　初茜（はつあかね、新年を表す）

3

Hatsu akane

hoshi dake to mita

asa no iro

The dark red of dawn on New Year's Day

I saw it only with stars

that morning color

Season word: *hatsu akane* (the dark red of dawn on New Year's Day; signifies the new year)

Stephen Yan

元日は

　　地平線の

　　　　向こうに待つ

がんじつは

　　ちへいせんの

　　　むこうにまつ

季語　　元日（がんじつ、新年）

Ganjitsu wa

chiheisen no

mukō ni matsu

The first day of the year

waits

beyond the horizon

Season word: *ganjitsu* (New Year's Day; new year)

Felicity Audet

この初日

　　昨夜の夢を

　　　　現実に

このはつひ

　　さくやのゆめを

　　　　げんじつに

季語　初日（はつひ、新年）

Kono hatsu hi

　　sakuya no yume o

　　　genjitsu ni

At this New Year's sunrise

　　I'll turn last night's dreams

　　　into reality

Season word: *hatsu hi* (sunrise on New Year's Day; new year)

Natalie Diaz

新年や

　　長〜い冬の

　　　　古くなる

しんねんや

　　なが〜いふゆの

　　　　ふるくなる

季語　新年（しんねん、新年）

Shin nen ya

　　nagāi fuyu no

　　　　furuku naru

The new year

　　The long winter

　　　　has become old

Season word: *shin nen* (new year; new year)

Anne Wen

初日の出

　　炉の前からの

　　　　幸せよ

はつひので

　　ろのまえからの

　　　　しあわせよ

季語　初日の出（はつひので、新年）

11

Hatsu hinode

ro no mae kara no

shiawase yo

The first sunrise

seen from in front of the furnace

makes one feel happy

Season word: *hatsu hinode* (sunrise on New Year's Day;

new year)

Felicity Audet

初空や

　　鮮やかなのに

　　　　ほろ苦い

はつぞらや

　　あざやかなのに

　　　　ほろにがい

季語　初空（はつぞら、新年）

Hatsu zora ya

    azayaka nano ni

       horo nigai

The year's first morning sky

    though vivid

       is bittersweet

Season word: *hatsu zora* (the morning sky on New Year's

Day; new year)

Natalie Diaz

新年や

　　花火の散って

　　　　家族散る

しんねんや

　　はなびのちって

　　　　かぞくちる

季語　　新年（しんねん、新年）

Shin nen ya

    hanabi no chitte

      kazoku chiru

The new year

    The firework fell

      Then the family moment is gone

Season word: *shin nen* (new year; new year)

Anne Wen

初夢や

　　寒い心を

　　　　温める

はつゆめや

　　さむいこころを

　　　　あたためる

季語　　初夢（はつゆめ、新年）

Hatsu yume ya

samui kokoro o

atatameru

The first dream of the year

warms

the cold heart

Season word: *hatsu yume* (first dream on the night of New

Year's Day; new year)

Felicity Audet

初凪の

　　旋風となる

　　　　人生よ

はつなぎの

　　せんぷうとなる

　　　　じんせいよ

季語　初凪（はつなぎ、新年）

Hatsu nagi no

senpū to naru

jinsei yo

From first calm sea

of the new year

a whirlwind life

Season word: *hatsu nagi* (the calm sea on New Year's

Day; new year)

Natalie Diaz

初夢を

    保つと機嫌

        舞い上がる

はつゆめを

    たもつときげん

        まいあがる

季語　初夢（はつゆめ、新年）

Hatsu yume o

    tamotsu to kigen

        mai agaru

I preserve

    my first dreams

        so my spirits soar

Season word: *hatsu yume* (first dream on the night of New Year's Day; new year)

Felicity Audet

寒の入

　　残った枝に

　　　　枯葉あり

かんのいり

　　のこったえだに

　　　　かれはあり

季語　寒の入（かんのいり、冬）

寒の入は、通常、1月6日となる。寒の明けは2月3日。

Kan no iri

nokōtta eda ni

kareha ari

The coldest season has started

The remaining branches

The dead leaves

Season word: *kan no iri* (beginning of the coldest season; winter)

Kan no iri (beginning of the coldest season) usually falls on January 6 and Kan no ake (end of the coldest season) ends on February 3, which marks the end of winter, as well.

Anne Wen

February

Photograph 2. Frozen Lake Carnegie

千鳥から

　　白い世界に

　　　　音のなし

ちどりから

　　しろいせかいに

　　　　おとのなし

季語　　千鳥(ちどり、冬)

27

Chidori kara

shiroi sekai ni

oto no nashi

In the white world

there is no sound

from the plover

Season word: *chidori* (plover; winter)

Felicity Audet

大きい木

　　小枝を見れば

　　　冬の梅

おおきいき

　　こえだをみれば

　　　ふゆのうめ

季語　冬の梅（ふゆのうめ、冬）

Ōkii ki

koeda o mireba

fuyu no ume

The big tree

Looking at the small branch

one finds the winter plum blossoms

Season word: *fuyu no ume* (winter plum blossoms; winter)

Henry Slater

節分や

　　雪の泣く音か

　　　　さえずりか

せつぶんや

　　ゆきのなくねか

　　　　さえずりか

季語　節分（せつぶん、2月3日、冬）

俳句では、2月4日（立春）から春となる。

31

Setsubun ya

yuki no naku ne ka

saezuri ka

The eve of the beginning of spring

is it the snow sobbing

or the bird chirping?

Season word: *setsubun* (eve of the beginning of spring,

February 3; winter)

In haiku, February 4 marks the beginning of spring.

Jacob Williams

里山に

　　早梅の咲く

　　　　春近し

さとやまに

　　はやうめのさく

　　　　はるちかし

季語　　早梅（はやうめ、冬）　春近し（はるちかし、冬）

Sato yama ni

haya ume no saku

haru chikashi

In the village

early plum blossoms appear

and spring is coming soon

Season words: *haya ume* (early plum blossoms; winter)

and *haru chikashi* (spring is coming soon; winter)

Felicity Audet

雪溶けて

　　春の始まり

　　　　まだ寒い

ゆきどけて

　　はるのはじまり

　　　　まださむい

季語　　雪溶け（ゆきどけ、春）　春の始め（はるのはじめ、
春）

Yuki dokete

haru no hajimari

mada samui

The snow is melting

Spring season started

Yet it is still cold

Season words: *yuki doke* (the snow melts; spring) and *haru no hajime* (beginning of spring)

Anne Wen

春の土

    雪解けなのに

        草のなし

はるのつち

    ゆきどけなのに

        くさのなし

季語　春の土（はるのつち、春）　雪解け（ゆきどけ、春）

Haru no tsuchi

yuki doke nano ni

kusa no nashi

The spring soil

Although the snow melts

there is no grass

Season words: *haru no tsuchi* (spring soil; spring) and *yuki doke* (the snow melts; spring)

Felicity Audet

雪解けや

　　小川は踊る

　　　　笑いつつ

ゆきどけや

　　おがわはおどる

　　　　わらいつつ

季語　雪解け（ゆきどけ、春）

Yuki doke ya

    ogawa wa odoru

        warai tsutsu

The snow melts

    the brook dances

        while laughing

Season word: *yuki doke* (the snow melts; spring)

Stephen Yan

春めきて

　　梅咲いている

　　　　一つずつ

はるめきて

　　うめさいている

　　　　ひとつずつ

季語　　春めく(はるめく、春)　梅(うめ、春)

41

Haru meki te

ume saite iru

hitotsu zutsu

The signs of spring

The plum is blooming

One by one

Season words: *haru meku* (signs of spring; spring) and *ume*

(plum blossom; spring)

Anne Wen

March

Photograph 3. Pear blossoms

余寒の日

　　ため息白い

　　　　もやとなる

よかんのひ

　　ためいきしろい

　　　　もやとなる

季語　　余寒の日（よかんのひ、春）

45

Yokan no hi

    tame iki shiroi

        moya to naru

On the lingering cold day

    my sighs

        become white mist

Season word: *yokan no hi* (day of lingering cold; spring)

Natalie Diaz

春一番

　　南より来る

　　　　われ踊る

はるいちばん

　　みなみよりくる

　　　　われおどる

季語　春一番（はるいちばん、春）

Haru ichiban

minami yori kuru

ware odoru

The first spring gust

came from the south

and I danced

Season word: *haru ichiban* (first spring gust; spring)

Felicity Audet

朝光や

　　椿のように

　　　　咲く笑顔

ちょうこうや

　　つばきのように

　　　　さくえがお

季語　椿（つばき、春）

Chōkō ya

tsubaki no yō ni

saku egao

Morning light

my smile blooms

like a camellia

Season word: *tsubaki* (camellia; spring)

Natalie Diaz

春の風邪

　　　学校は無理

　　　　　休もうね

はるのかぜ

　　　がっこうはむり

　　　　　やすもうね

季語　　春の風邪（はるのかぜ、春）

Haru no kaze

gakkō wa muri

yasumō ne

A spring cold

No school today

Time to rest

Season word: *haru no kaze* (spring cold; spring)

Henry Slater

April

Photograph 4. Cherry blossoms in the rain

春の雪

　　四月の初め

　　　　寒すぎる

はるのゆき

　　しがつのはじめ

　　　　さむすぎる

季語　春の雪（はるのゆき、春）　四月（しがつ、春）

Haru no yuki

Shigatsu no hajime

samu sugiru

Snow in the spring

It's the beginning of April

It's too cold

Season words: *haru no yuki* (spring snow; spring) and

Shigatsu (April; spring)

Henry Slater

花曇り

　　　小雨の降りて

　　　　　花の泡

はなぐもり

　　　こさめのふりて

　　　　　はなのあわ

季語　花曇り（はなぐもり、春）

Hana gumori

    kosame no furite

        hana no awa

The cloudy day in the cherry blossom season

    the light rain falls

        and the flower petals become bubbles

Season word: *hana gumori* (a cloudy day in the cherry

blossom season; spring)

Natalie Diaz

春空や

　　漂う雲を

　　　　風揺らす

はるぞらや

　　ただようくもを

　　　　かぜゆらす

季語　春空（はるぞら、春）

Haru zora ya

dadayou kumo o

kaze yurasu

Spring sky

the floating cloud

the wind swings it

Season word: *haru zora* (spring sky; spring)

Stephen Yan

春の雨

　　はらはら落ちる

　　　　花びらよ

はるのあめ

　　はらはらおちる

　　　　はなびらよ

季語　　春の雨（はるのあめ、春）

61

Haru no ame

    hara hara ochiru

        hana bira yo

The spring rain

    The flower petals

        are dripping gently

Season word: *haru no ame* (spring rain; spring)

Natalie Diaz

桜咲く

　　花びら落ちて

　　　　空の泣く

さくらさく

　　はなびらおちて

　　　　そらのなく

季語　桜(さくら、春)

Sakura saku

    hana bira ochite

        sora no naku

The cherry blooms

    the flower petals fall

        and the sky weeps

Season word: *sakura* (cherry blossoms; spring)

Anne Wen

風光る

　　虹色の凧

　　　　踊りたり

かぜひかる

　　にじいろのたこ

　　　　おどりたり

季語　風光る（かぜひかる、春）　凧（たこ、春）

Kaze hikaru

    niji iro no tako

        odori tari

The wind shines

    making the rainbow-colored kite

        dance

Season words: *kaze hikaru* (the wind shines; spring) and

tako (kite; spring)

Natalie Diaz

May

Photograph 5. Bleeding heart flowers

日本晴れ

　　陽光の種

　　　　ふわり蒔く

にほんばれ

　　ようこうのたね

　　　　ふわりまく

季語　種蒔き(たねまき、春)

Nihon bare

yōkō no tane

fuwari maku

A beautiful day

seeds of sunshine

are scattered tenderly

Season word: *tane maki* (to sow seeds; spring)

Jacob Williams

きれいな日

　　公園に行く

　　　　百千鳥

きれいなひ

　　こうえんにいく

　　　　ももちどり

季語　百千鳥（ももちどり、春）

Kirei na hi

kōen ni iku

momo chidori

A beautiful day

We go to the park

and hear hundreds of beautiful birds calling

Season word: *momo chidori* (hundreds of migrating birds

chirping; spring)

Henry Slater

72

木漏れ日や

　　緑の蝶が

　　　　飛び回る

こもれびや

　　みどりのちょうが

　　　　とびまわる

季語　蝶(ちょう、春)

Komore bi ya

midori no chō ga

tobi mawaru

Sunlight through the forest canopy—

the fluttering

of green butterflies

Season word: *chō* (butterfly; spring)

Jacob Williams

五月雨に

　　赤い傘咲く

　　　　芥子のよう

さみだれに

　　あかいかささく

　　　　けしのよう

季語　五月雨（さみだれ、夏）　芥子（けし、夏）

俳句では、5月5日（立夏）から夏となる。

Samidare ni

    akai kasa saku

        keshi no yō

In the early summer rain

    red umbrellas bloom

        like poppies

Season words: *samidare* (early summer rain; summer) and *keshi* (poppy; summer)

In haiku, May 5 marks the beginning of summer.

Jacob Williams

June

Photograph 6. "Water Lilies and Japanese Bridge (1899)"

by Claude Monet, Princeton University Art Museum

夏の夜

　　蛍が飛ぶよ

　　　　キラキラと

なつのよる

　　ほたるがとぶよ

　　　　キラキラと

季語　夏の夜（なつのよる、夏）　蛍（ほたる、夏）

Natsu no yoru

    hotaru ga tobu yo

        kira kira to

In the summer night

    fireflies fly

        twinkling

Season words: *natsu no yoru* (summer night; summer) and *hotaru* (firefly; summer)

Felicity Audet

あの星に

　　願ってみたが

　　　　蛍なり

あのほしに

　　ねがってみたが

　　　　ほたるなり

季語　　蛍（ほたる、夏）

81

Ano hoshi ni

    negatte mita ga

        hotaru nari

I tried to wish

    upon that star

        but it was a firefly

Season word: *hotaru* (firefly; summer)

Natalie Diaz

星空や

　　蛍のワルツ

　　　　映すよう

ほしぞらや

　　ほたるのワルツ

　　　　うつすよう

季語　蛍（ほたる、夏）

Hoshi zora ya

　　hotaru no warutsu

　　　　utsusu yō

The starlit night

　　and the waltz of fireflies—

　　　　are they reflections?

Season word: *hotaru* (firefly; summer)

Jacob Williams

夏空や

　　雲の間に

　　　　虹の赤

なつぞらや

　　くものあいだに

　　　　にじのあか

季語　夏空（なつぞら、夏）　虹（にじ、夏）

Natsu zora ya

kumo no aida ni

niji no aka

In the summer sky

Between the clouds

I see red in the rainbow

Season words: *natsu zora* (summer sky; summer) and *niji*

(rainbow; summer)

Anne Wen

踊ろうか

　　短夜なのに

　　　　月綺麗

おどろうか

　　みじかよなのに

　　　　つききれい

季語　短夜（みじかよ、夏）

Odorō ka

mijika yo nano ni

tsuki kirei

Shall we dance?

Though the summer night is short

the moon is beautiful

Season word: *mijika yo* (short summer night; summer)

Natalie Diaz

朝曇り

　　真珠の色の

　　　　天光る

あさぐもり

　　しんじゅのいろの

　　　　てんひかる

季語　　朝曇り（あさぐもり、夏）

Asa gumori

shinju no iro no

ten hikaru

The hazy summer morning

The color of pearl

shines in the heavens

Season word: *asa gumori* (hazy summer morning; summer)

Jacob Williams

July

Photograph 7. Seashells

サングラスより

　　君の目と

　　　　雲の峰

サングラスより

　　きみのめと

　　　　くものみね

季語　サングラス（夏）　雲の峰（くものみね、夏）

San gurasu yori

kimi no me to

kumo no mine

From my sunglasses—

your eyes and

billowing clouds

Season words: *san gurasu* (sunglasses; summer) and *kumo no mine* (billowing clouds, cumulonimbus clouds; summer)

Jacob Williams

天空や

　　油彩のような

　　　　雲の峰

てんくうや

　　ゆさいのような

　　　　くものみね

季語　雲の峰(くものみね、夏)

Tenkū ya

    yusai no yō na

        kumo no mine

In the high sky

    the towering cloud

        looks like an oil painting

Season word: *kumo no mine* (towering cloud,

cumulonimbus cloud; summer)

Natalie Diaz

浜涼み

　　　頬に花塩

　　　　　海のキス

はますずみ

　　　ほほにはなじお

　　　　　うみのキス

季語　　涼み(すずみ、夏)

Hama suzumi

hoho ni hana jio

umi no kisu

Cooling in the breeze at the beach

traces of salt on the cheek

the ocean's kiss

Season word: *suzumi* (cooling off; summer)

Jacob Williams

今日炎暑

　　顔に太陽

　　　　明日もまた

きょうえんしょ

　　かおにたいよう

　　　　あすもまた

季語　炎暑（えんしょ、夏）

Kyō ensho

kao ni taiyō

asu mo mata

Today is fiery hot

The sun shines on my face

Tomorrow the same repeats

Season word: *ensho* (burning hot; summer)

Anne Wen

日盛りや

　　地が無定形

　　　　空となる

ひざかりや

　　ちがむていけい

　　　　そらとなる

季語　日盛り（ひざかり、夏）

Hi zakari ya

chi ga mu teikei

sora to naru

At the hottest time of the day

the earth is shapeless

and becomes air

Season word: *hi zakari* (the hottest time of the day;

summer)

Jacob Williams

アロハシャツ

　　飛行機に乗る

　　　　楽しみだ

アロハシャツ

　　ひこうきにのる

　　　　たのしみだ

季語　アロハシャツ（夏）

Aroha shatsu

hikōki ni noru

tanoshimi da

With my Hawaiian shirt

I get on the plane

Very excited

Season word: *Aroha shatsu* (Hawaiian shirt; summer)

Henry Slater

夏みかん

　　水分多く

　　　　必要よ

なつみかん

　　すいぶんおおく

　　　　ひつようよ

季語　夏みかん(なつみかん、夏)

Natsu mikan

suibun ōku

hitsuyō yo

Summer oranges

Contain a lot of water

That is very necessary

Season word: *natsu mikan* (*lit.*, "summer mikan," summer

daidai orange, *citrus natsudaidai*; summer)

Anne Wen

お買い物

　　友達と行く

　　　　パパイヤだ

おかいもの

　　ともだちといく

　　　　パパイヤだ

季語　パパイヤ（夏）

O kaimono

tomodachi to iku

papaiya da

Going shopping

With my friend

There's a papaya!

Season word: *papaiya* (papaya; summer)

Henry Slater

August

Photograph 8. Sunflowers

ひまわりが

　　大きくなるよ

　　　　幸せよ

ひまわりが

　　おおきくなるよ

　　　　しあわせよ

季語　　ひまわり(夏)

Himawari ga

    ōkiku naru yo

        shiawase yo

Sunflowers

    grow bigger

        I am happy

Season word: *himawari* (sunflower; summer)

Felicity Audet

外に出て

　　汗がくっつく

　　　　秋を待つ

そとにでて

　　あせがくっつく

　　　　あきをまつ

季語　汗（あせ、夏）　秋を待つ（あきをまつ、夏）

Soto ni dete

    ase ga kuttsuku

       aki o matsu

I go outside

    The sweat sticks to me

       I'm waiting for autumn

Season words: *ase* (sweat; summer) and *aki o matsu* (to wait for autumn; summer)

Henry Slater

友達と

　　花火を見てる

　　　　楽しいよ

ともだちと

　　はなびをみてる

　　　　たのしいよ

季語　花火（はなび、夏）

Tomodachi to

    hanabi o miteru

        tanoshii yo

With friends

    I watch fireworks

        It is fun

Season word: *hanabi* (firework; summer)

Felicity Audet

砂漠雨

　　そして日暮れに

　　　　白い夜顔

さばくあめ

　　そしてひぐれに

　　　　しろいよるがお

季語　夜顔（よるがお、秋）

俳句では、8月7日（立秋）から秋となる。

Sabaku ame

    soshite higure ni

        shiroi yoru gao

Desert rain

    Then in the evening

        White moonflowers

Season word: *yoru gao* (moonflower; autumn)

In haiku, August 7 marks the beginning of autumn.

Jacob Williams

朝明けや

　　萎む夕顔

　　　　置き手紙

あさあけや

　　しぼむゆうがお

　　　　おきてがみ

季語　　夕顔（ゆうがお、この句の場合、夜顔をさす、秋）

夕顔は北アフリカ及びインド原産のウリ科の植物。夜顔は

アメリカ熱帯地方・亜熱帯地方原産の砂漠地帯の植物。

共に、夕方から白い花を咲かせることから、夜顔は、夕顔

と呼ばれることもある。

Asa ake ya

    shibomu yūgao

        oki tegami

It's daybreak

    and the withering moonflowers

        are farewell letters

Season word: *yūgao* (actually *yoru gao*, moonflower; autumn)

Yoru gao (moonflower, tropical white morning-glory) is a desert plant native to tropical and subtropical regions of America. By contrast, yūgao (white-flowered gourd) is a plant native to North Africa and India. The two plants are not related to each other. However, due to the resemblance in their nocturnal-blooming white flowers, yoru gao is sometimes referred to as yūgao.

Jacob Williams

天の川

　　泳ぐ星たち

　　　　行き来する

あまのがわ

　　およぐほしたち

　　　　いききする

季語　天の川（あまのがわ、秋）

Ama no gawa

    oyogu hoshi tachi

      iki ki suru

In the Milky Way

    the swimming stars

      come and go

Season word: *ama no gawa* (Milky Way; autumn)

Natalie Diaz

コオロギや

　　竹から歌う

　　　　立秋よ

コオロギや

　　たけからうたう

　　　　りっしゅうよ

季語　コオロギ（秋）　立秋（りっしゅう、8月7日、秋）

Kōrogi ya

    take kara utau

        risshū yo

Crickets

    sing from the bamboo

        autumn has come

Season words: *kōrogi* (cricket; autumn) and *risshū* (arrival of autumn, August 7; autumn)

Felicity Audet

124

September

Photograph 9. Sunset reflections on Lake Carnegie

秋の朝

　　ドアを開けると

　　　　風が吹く

あきのあさ

　　ドアをあけると

　　　　かぜがふく

季語　　秋の朝（あきのあさ、秋）

Aki no asa

doa o akeru to

kaze ga fuku

Autumn morning

I open the door

Wind blows inside

Season word: *aki no asa* (autumn morning; autumn)

Anne Wen

初嵐

　　紫紺雲海

　　　　夜支配せり

はつあらし

　　しこんうんかい

　　　　よるしはいせり

季語　初嵐（はつあらし、秋）

雲海は夏の季語であるが、この句の場合は、四字熟語の一部であり、季語として使われていない。

Hatsu arashi

shikon unkai

yoru shihai seri

The first autumn storm

a violet sea of clouds

rules over the night

Season word: *hatsu arashi* (first autumn storm; autumn)

Unkai (sea of clouds) is a season word of summer; however, in this haiku, it is not used as such, but it is a part of a four-character phrase.

Jacob Williams

三日月や

　　ファイン・ホールの

　　　　窓明り

みかづきや

　　ファイン・ホールの

　　　　まどあかり

季語　三日月（みかづき、秋）

ファイン・ホールは、プリンストン大学の数学部の所在する

建物。キャンパスで、最も高い建造物である。

Mika zuki ya

Fain Hōru no

mado akari

The waxing crescent

The windows on Fine Hall

Are brightly light

Season word: *mika zuki* (third-night moon; autumn)

Fine Hall refers to the building of Princeton University's Mathematics Department, a tower which is the tallest on campus.

Stephen Yan

暁や

　　露に日差しの

　　　　輝ける

あかつきや

　　つゆにひざしの

　　　　かがやける

季語　　露（つゆ、秋）

Akatsuki ya

tsuyu ni hizashi no

kagayakeru

At dawn

the sunshine is reflected

on the dewdrops

Season word: *tsuyu* (dewdrops; autumn)

Felicity Audet

一斉に

　　つくつく法師

　　　　喋ってる

いっせいに

　　つくつくぼうし

　　　　しゃべってる

季語　つくつく法師（つくつくぼうし、法師蝉、ホウシゼミ、秋）

Issei ni

    tsuku tsuku bōshi

        shabette ru

The Walker's cicadas

    are chattering

        all at once

Season word: *tsuku tsuku bōshi* (Walker's cicadas;

autumn)

Natalie Diaz

秋の夜

　　月が昇るよ

　　　　皆静か

あきのよる

　　つきがのぼるよ

　　　　みなしずか

季語　秋の夜（あきのよる、秋）　月（つき、秋）

Aki no yoru

    tsuki ga noboru yo

        mina shizuka

Autumn night

    The moon is rising

        Silent around us

Season words: *aki no yoru* (**autumn night**; autumn) and *tsuki* (**moon**; autumn)

Anne Wen

月光や

　　辞書と教科書

　　　　秋浴びる

げっこうや

　　じしょときょうかしょ

　　　　あきあびる

季語　　月光（げっこう、秋）　秋（あき、秋）

Gekkō ya

jisho to kyōkasho

aki abiru

Beneath the moonlight

The dictionary and textbook lie

Bathing in Autumn

Season words: *gekkō* (moonlight; autumn) and *aki*

(autumn; autumn)

Stephen Yan

秋の色

　　逍遥するや

　　　　神隠し

あきのいろ

　　しょうようするや

　　　　かみかくし

季語　秋の色（あきのいろ、秋）

Aki no iro

    shōyō suru ya

        kami kakushi

Strolling in the scenery

    of the fall color;

        a spiriting away

Season word: *aki no iro* (scenery of the fall color; autumn)

Natalie Diaz

142

October

Photograph 10. Ivy fall foliage

高いビル

　　下から上に

　　　　伸びる蔦

たかいビル

　　したからうえに

　　　　のびるつた

季語　蔦（つた、秋）

Takai biru

    shita kara ue ni

        nobiru tsuta

Tall buildings

    From bottom to top

        The ivy gets taller

Season word: *tsuta* (ivy; autumn)

Henry Slater

秋深し

　　りんごシャキシャキ

　　　爽やかだ

あきふかし

　　りんごシャキシャキ

　　　さわやかだ

季語　　秋深し（あきふかし、秋）　りんご（リンゴ、秋）

147

Aki fukashi

   ringo shaki shaki

      sawayaka da

In late autumn

   the crisp apple

      is refreshing

Season words: *aki fukashi* (*lit.*, "deep autumn," late autumn; autumn) and *ringo* (apple, autumn)

Felicity Audet

朝の街

　　紅葉あふれる

　　　　青山通り

あさのまち

　　もみじあふれる

　　　　あおやまどおり

季語　　紅葉（もみじ、秋）

Asa no machi

   momiji afureru

      Aoyama dōri

The city in the morning

   Falling leaves everywhere

      On Aoyama Avenue

Season word: *momiji* (maple fall foliage; autumn)

Henry Slater

そよ風に

　　紅葉が噂を

　　　　ささやいた

そよかぜに

　　もみじがうわさを

　　　　ささやいた

季語　紅葉(もみじ、秋)

Soyo kaze ni

    momiji ga uwasa o

        sasayai ta

To the breeze

    The maple fall foliage

        whispers a rumor

Season word: *momiji* (maple fall foliage; autumn)

Felicity Audet

爽やかに

　　木から落ちる葉

　　　　色変える

さわやかに

　　きからおちるは

　　　　いろかえる

季語　　爽やか（さわやか、秋）

Sawayaka ni

ki kara ochiru ha

iro kaeru

Outside there is refreshing air

Leaves fall from tree

Colors are changing

Season word: *sawayaka* (refreshing autumn air: autumn)

Anne Wen

重い梨

　　　枝を垂れさせ

　　　　　呼び出すよ

おもいなし

　　　えだをたれさせ

　　　　　よびだすよ

季語　梨(なし、秋)

155

Omoi nashi

    eda o tare sase

      yobi dasu yo

The heavy pears

    hanging from the branches

      call out to me

Season word: *nashi* (pear; autumn)

Felicity Audet

朝寒や

　　イー・クアドへ

　　　「独り旅」

あさざむや

　　イー・クアドへ

　　　ひとりたび

季語　朝寒（あさざむ、秋）

イー・クアドは、プリンストン大学の工学部の所在する建物。

キャンパスで最も遠い場所にあることから、学生は、イー・

クアドへ行くことを「旅」と呼んでいる。

Asa zamu ya

Ii Quado e

hitori tabi

The cold morning air

One journeys to the E-Quad,

A Solitary Path

Season word: *asa zamu* (cold morning; autumn)

E-Quad stands for the Engineering Quadrangle, which houses Princeton University's Engineering Department. Being the farthest point on campus, travelling to E-Quad is often jokingly likened by students to a journey.

Stephen Yan

北の空

　　　カシオペア座は

　　　　　きれいだな

きたのそら

　　　カシオペアざは

　　　　　きれいだな

季語　　カシオペア座（カシオペアざ、秋）

Kita no sora

   Kashiopea za wa

      kirei dana

The northern sky

   Cassiopeia shines

      What a pretty sight

Season word: *Kashiopea za* (constellation Cassiopeia; autumn)

Henry Slater

寒蛩や

　　名残の秋の

　　　　レクイエム

かんきょうや

　　なごりのあきの

　　　　レクイエム

季語　寒蛩（かんきょう、秋）

寒蛩（かんきょう）とは、晩秋に寂しげに鳴くコオロギのこと。

Kankyō ya

    nagori no aki no

        rekuiemu

The feeble chorus

    of crickets chirping—

        a requiem for the remnants of autumn

Season word: *kankyō* (feebly chirping crickets; autumn)

Jacob Williams

November

Photograph 11. Maple fall foliage on the snow

昨夜見た

　　満天の星

　　　今朝の霜

さくやみた

　　まんてんのほし

　　　けさのしも

季語　霜(しも、冬)

俳句では、11月7日(立冬)から冬となる。

Saku ya mita

    man ten no hoshi

       kesa no shimo

The starry ocean

    That filled yesterday's night sky

       Is the morning's frost

Season word: *shimo* (frost; winter)

In haiku, November 7 marks the beginning of winter.

Stephen Yan

朝早く

　　窓から見ると

　　　　初雪だ

あさはやく

　　まどからみると

　　　　はつゆきだ

季語　初雪（はつゆき、冬）

Asa hayaku

    mado kara miruto

      hatsu yuki da

Early in the morning

    Looking out the window

      The first snow

Season word: *hatsu yuki* (first snow of the season; winter)

Henry Slater

窓の霜

　　道わきの雪

　　　　みな静か

まどのしも

　　みちわきのゆき

　　　　みなしずか

季語　霜（しも、冬）　雪（ゆき、冬）

Mado no shimo

    michi waki no yuki

        mina shizuka

Frost on the window

    Piles of snow by the street

        Silence surrounds us

Season words: *shimo* (frost; winter) and *yuki* (snow; winter)

Anne Wen

塾帰り

　　　両手ですする

　　　　　　缶コーヒー

じゅくがえり

　　　りょうてですする

　　　　　　かんコーヒー

季語　缶コーヒー（かんコーヒー、冬）

Juku gaeri

    ryōte de susuru

        kan kōhii

On the way back from the cram school

    one sips a hot canned coffee

        with two hands

Season word: *kan kōhii* (hot canned coffee; winter)

Kouta Ohyama

雪の花

　　周りどこにも

　　　そっと降る

ゆきのはな

　　まわりどこにも

　　　そっとふる

季語　雪の花（ゆきのはな、冬）

Yuki no hana

      mawari doko nimo

          sotto furu

Flurries of snow

      Everywhere around me

          Softly fall down

Season word: *yuki no hana* (snowflakes; winter)

Anne Wen

木枯らしや

　　窓ガタガタと

　　　　震えたり

こがらしや

　　まどガタガタと

　　　　ふるえたり

季語　木枯らし（こがらし、冬）

Ko garashi ya

    mado gata gata to

        furue tari

In the winter gale

    the windows

        rattle

Season word: *ko garashi* (winter gale; winter)

Natalie Diaz

「リスでっか！」

　　スマホまさぐる

　　　　手袋よ

「リスでっか！」

　　スマホまさぐる

　　　　てぶくろよ

季語　手袋(てぶくろ、冬)

177

"Risu dekka!"

    sumaho masaguru

        tebukuro yo

"What a big squirrel!"

    a glove is searching

        for a smart phone

Season word: *te bukuro* (gloves; winter)

Kouta Ohyama

凍て風や

　　　答えのなく

　　　　　沈黙する

いてかぜや

　　　こたえのなく

　　　　　ちんもくする

季語　凍て風（いてかぜ、冬）

Ite kaze ya

    kotae no naku

        chinmoku suru

The freezing wind

    No response

        Silence

Season word: *ite kaze* (freezing wind; winter)

Anne Wen

雪よまた

　　君の足跡

　　　　真似てみる

ゆきよまた

　　きみのあしあと

　　　　まねてみる

季語　　雪（ゆき、冬）

Yuki yo mata

    kimi no ashiato

        manete miru

Again

    I trace your footprints

        in the snow

Season word: *yuki* (snow; winter)

Natalie Diaz

霜降る音

　　煌めく空へ

　　　　響くかな

しもふるおと

　　きらめくそらへ

　　　　ひびくかな

季語　霜（しも、冬）

Shimo furu oto

kirameku sora e

hibiku kana

The sound of frost falling

It reverberates

Through the sparkling sky

Season word: *shimo* (frost; winter)

Stephen Yan

December

Photograph 12. Winter sun

冬の山

　　　空は水色

　　　　静かな日

ふゆのやま

　　　そらはみずいろ

　　　　しずかなひ

季語　冬の山（ふゆのやま、冬）

Fuyu no yama

    sora wa mizu iro

        shizuka na hi

The winter mountain

    the sky is in water color

        on the quiet day

Season word: *fuyu no yama* (winter mountain; winter)

Henry Slater

朝光や

　　真白を被り

　　　　山眠る

ちょうこうや

　　ましろをかぶり

　　　　やまねむる

季語　　山眠る（やまねむる、冬）

189

Chōkō ya

mashiro o kaburi

yama nemuru

The early twilight glow

Blanketed in pure white

The mountain sleeps

Season word: *yama nemuru* (the mountain sleeps; winter)

Stephen Yan

名古屋着

　　木枯らし運ぶ

　　　　鰹出汁

なごやちゃく

　　こがらしはこぶ

　　　　かつおだし

季語　木枯らし（こがらし、冬）

名古屋駅の新幹線のプラットホームには、有名なうどんの
立ち食い店があり、乗降客で賑わっている。

Nagoya chaku

　　ko garashi hakobu

　　　　katsuo dashi

The bullet train arrives at Nagoya Station

　　the wintry wind

　　　　delivers the scent of the bonito noodle broth

Season word: *ko garashi* (wintry wind; winter)

On the platform of the Shinkansen train at Nagoya Station

has a famous udon noodle stand, crowded with passengers

departing from Nagoya or getting off at Nagoya.

Kouta Ohyama

床に囲碁

　　一家炉辺に

　　　　揃いたり

ゆかにいご

　　いっかろばたに

　　　　そろいたり

季語　炉辺（ろばた、冬）

Yuka ni igo

ikka robata ni

soroi tari

The igo board game on the floor

the whole family gathered

in front of the fireplace

Season word: *robata* (fireplace; winter)

Stephen Yan

クリスマス

　　　外は寒いね

　　　　　家族は一緒

クリスマス

　　　そとはさむいね

　　　　　かぞくはいっしょ

季語　　クリスマス(冬)

Kurisumasu

soto wa samui ne

kazoku wa issho

Christmas

it is cold outside

the family is together

Season word: *Kurisumasu* (Christmas; winter)

Henry Slater

京都駅

　　ツリーに映える

　　　　真っ赤な手

きょうとえき

　　ツリーにはえる

　　　　まっかなて

季語　　ツリー（クリスマス・ツリー、冬）

Kyoto eki

tsurii ni haeru

makka na te

Kyoto Station

the red hands are reflected

on the Christmas tree ornaments

Season word: *tsurii* (Christmas tree; winter)

Shiina Yuri

数え日や

　　時間数える

　　　　分と秒

かぞえびや

　　じかんかぞえる

　　　　ふんとびょう

季語　数え日（かぞえび、冬）

Kazoebi ya

   jikan kazo eru

      fun to byō

Counting the days

   The hours

      The minutes and seconds

Season word: *kazoe bi* (counting the days until New Year's

Day; winter/yearend)

Anne Wen

クリスマス

　　部屋に溢れる

　　　　プレゼント

クリスマス

　　へやにあふれる

　　　　プレゼント

季語　　クリスマス(冬)

201

Kurisumasu

heya ni afureru

purezento

Christmastime

The room overflowing with

presents

Season word: *Kurisumasu* (Christmastime; winter)

Henry Slater

202

年の市

　　　元気いっぱい

　　　　　人多い

としのいち

　　　げんきいっぱい

　　　　　ひとおおい

季語　年の市（としのいち、冬・暮）

Toshi no ichi

    genki ippai

        hito ōi

The yearend market

    Full of energy

        With many people

Season word: *toshi no ichi* (yearend market to prepare for

New Year's Day celebration; winter/yearend)

Anne Wen

年の暮れ

　　回想したり

　　　　微笑んだり

としのくれ

　　かいそうしたり

　　　　ほほえんだり

季語　年の暮れ（としのくれ、冬・暮）

Toshi no kure

    kaisō shitari

        hohoen dari

At the year's end

    I reminisced

        and smiled

Season word: *toshi no kure* (year's end; winter/yearend)

Natalie Diaz

大晦日

　　笑い声鳴る

　　　　ゲラゲラと

おおみそか

　　わらいごえなる

　　　　ゲラゲラと

季語　大晦日（おおみそか、冬・暮）

Ō misoka

    warai goe naru

        gera gera to

New Year's Eve

    The sound of laughter

        And giggles ring

Season word: *Ō-misoka* (New Year's Eve; winter/yearend)

Anne Wen

大晦日

　　今年も終わる

　　　　もう少し

おおみそか

　　ことしもおわる

　　　　もうすこし

季語　大晦日（おおみそか、冬・暮）

Ō misoka

    kotoshi mo owaru

      mō sukoshi

New Year's Eve

    This year is going to end

      very soon

Season word: *Ō-misoka* (New Year's Eve; winter/yearend)

Henry Slater

List of Contributors

Felicity Audet, a sophomore '21, is pursing a degree in East Asian Studies. In her free time, she enjoys learning about photography and digital media, in addition to being an accomplished dancer and a prolific choreographer for dance groups on campus, including the acclaimed Princeton University Ballet.

Natalie Diaz is a senior '19.

ナタリーや予期せぬが好きこのように

Natalie '19 / enjoys the unexpected /...such as this haiku! She is studying computer science and linguistics, and she's going to miss Princeton a lot more than she thought she would.

Kouta Ohyama, a senior '19, is an international student from Tokyo, Japan, majoring in public policy in the Woodrow Wilson School. He plays a leadership role in various student organizations on campus, including the American Whig-Cliosophic Society (the oldest debate union in the United States whose origin goes back to James Madison, Aaron Burr Jr, and others), the U.S.-China Coalition, the Japanese Students Association (former president), and the Princeton University Band.

Henry Slater is a member of the Class of 2022. Having been born and raised in Tokyo, he speaks Japanese fluently. He also speaks some French and Wolof, which he learned from his year in Senegal through Princeton's Bridge Year Program. He is interested in human rights, social justice, creative writing, politics, and lots of other things, constantly learning and doing his best to keep an open mind.

Anne Wen is a freshman '22 from the island of Guam, planning to minor in Japanese. On campus, she is involved with Christian, entrepreneurship, and education efforts.

Influenced by her Japanese-speaking parents, her affinity for Japanese started in high school and continues in college. She spends her free time admiring mainland America: the metros, the concept of Fahrenheit, and most excitingly, snow!

Jacob Williams is a junior '20 in the Comparative Literature Department, pursuing certificates in Musical Performance and East Asian Studies. He is a member of the prestigious and venerable Princeton University Orchestra, playing the French horn, as well as a member and Social Chair of the Princeton Chamber Music Society. In his leisure time, he enjoys doing research, going to the gym, and spending time outdoors. He is going to visit Japan this summer to study Japanese and do research for his senior thesis.

Stephen Yan is a sophomore '21 from East Brunswick, New Jersey, majoring in Physics. In his spare time, Stephen enjoys creating pottery, rock climbing, hiking, and playing the piano (in addition to writing haikus). Stephen also watches anime and plays video games such as the Legend of Zelda, Starcraft, and League of Legends. He is going to visit the University of Tokyo this summer, sponsored by the Princeton Plasma Physics Laboratory (PPPL).

Shiina Yuri, a sophomore '21, is an international student from Kyoto, Japan. She studies public policy in the Woodrow Wilson School, and is interested in studying criminology and psychology as well. She is a member of the Japanese Students Association (incumbent president) and a keyboardist of the Princeton University Rock Ensemble. She is going to visit China this summer and then is going to study at Cambridge University for the 2019–2020 academic year.

Mayumi Itoh (editor) is a former professor of Political Science at the University of Nevada, Las Vegas. She has previously taught at Princeton University and Queens College, City University of New York, and has written numerous books and academic journal articles.